Constructive Classroom Behavior

A TEACHER'S GUIDE TO MODELING
AND ROLE-PLAYING TECHNIQUES

by
Irwin G. Sarason, Ph.D.
Barbara R. Sarason, Ph.D.

Behavioral Publications
New York
1974

CONTENTS

3 /19/74   Red.   2, 9 r

PREFACE

This manual is a companion to an earlier one, Reinforcing Productive Classroom Behavior, that dealt with the use of reinforcement procedures by school personnel as a means for shaping constructive behavior in children. The present pamphlet continues to focus on the behavior influence process, but its topic is modeling and role-playing as applied to classroom settings. As an object of scientific inquiry, the history of modeling and role-playing is shorter than that of operant conditioning. Nonetheless, their educational implications already have stimulated·both general excitement and the development of specific techniques that are relevant to pressing problems in the classroom.

Modeling and role-playing are profoundly important components of child development. Modeling is a process by which responses are acquired through observing the behavior of someone else (the model). When people role-play they enact social roles other than their own. This manual was written to help school personnel use modeling and role-playing in productive ways. Its intended readers will include teachers, teachers in training, counselors, and administrators. Its development was guided by both educators and research workers. Although more basic research in modeling is needed, it is clear that it can have powerful impacts and that these can be either for good or ill. This pamphlet describes how modeling can be used to achieve desirable goals. It summarizes the literature on modeling and discusses how teachers and other personnel in the schools can use modeling for the benefit of students.

ACKNOWLEDGMENTS

The preparation of this manual was made possible under a contract (OEG-0-72-4360 Project No. RO 20388) awarded by the United States Office of Education, Department of Health, Education, & Welfare, to the Human Interaction Research Institute (HIRI) Los Angeles, California. Edward M. Glaser, president of HIRI, was both supportive and facilitative throughout the period during which the manuscript was written. We are deeply indebted to him.

We were helped by many people. Several persons provided ideas, criticisms, and suggestions that contributed significantly to the manuscript. We thank the many teachers, counselors, and school psychologists who read and commented upon earlier drafts. Their number is too great to permit acknowledging individually the help given by the manuscript reviewers, but we appreciate all that they did.

The following persons were especially helpful to us at many points in the development of this manuscript: Albert Bandura, Roberta B. Barr, Paula Benzel, Maurice F. Freehill, Victor J. Ganzer, Kathalee Garrison, Jesse Gordon, Joy Hammersla, Norris G. Haring, Madeline Hunter, Davis Ja, Molly Lewin, Karol Marshall, Merle L. Meacham, Mary Alice Norman, Ted Rosenthal, Dorothea M. Ross, Ronald E. Smith, Jerome Stumphauzer, Melvin Sorcher, Carl E. Thoresen, Norma Tropp, Goodwin Watson, Carol K. Whalen, and C. Gilbert Wrenn.

I. INTRODUCTION

" . . . Models Don't Just Have Shapely Legs?"

Rich Harris was 45, Fran Hardy 25. They both worked at Central High School. Fran taught classes in English and drama; Rich taught social studies. They liked their work, liked having contact with kids, and both were challenged by problems at Central, a high school in an area of high population density, high unemployment -- and low morale.

Rich and Fran frequently ate together in the lunch room and took coffee breaks at the same time, often engaging in light conversation. Among their conversations were discussions about Central and its students, especially those who seemed lacking in academic motivation. The frequency of these discussions had increased in recent months as they became more deeply concerned about the direction in which Central seemed to be moving. Rich and Fran didn't mind problems, but they wished they could find answers with more facility.

A breakthrough occurred one afternoon as they visited in the teachers' lounge after school with some of their colleagues. Rich had just read a magazine article about a government-funded study dealing with the effects of television on viewers' behavior. "Children especially," he explained to the others, "try to copy the behavior of their TV heroes and heroines. You know, the boys begin acting like big shots. The article said TV and movie heroes act as models for some of those who watch them."

"You mean models don't just have shapely legs?" asked Marie Hilton, the art teacher.

Rich laughed. "Some do, Marie, but I was thinking of a different kind of model. Remember Linda Bolton last year? When she started using drugs, half the girls in her group followed her example."

The assembled teachers groaned in agreement. They remembered all too well.

"Say, I can give you a good example of that," said Skip Tennyson, the math teacher. "The first class I had right after I left school was teaching third grade in a mining town in eastern Pennsylvania. One of my students was Bobby, a sturdy little kid, freckles all over his face, good-natured most of the time, but very stubborn when he got his back up. One day he came in late, and it was about the tenth time in a row. You know how it is when you're new. I'd let it go too long. Anyhow, this time I decided to send him to the principal. He stood up beside his seat, holding his lunch box in his hand, and he glowered at me. I can remember as if it just happened yesterday. 'I ain't going to the principal,' he said, 'I quit!' and he marched out the door. I can't prove it, but I'll bet his father had boasted to his family many times about how he wouldn't take anything off any boss, he'd quit first."

"Like father, like son," said Mary Clay from the back of the room where she was grading social studies papers. Rich was surprised because he'd thought she wasn't even listening.

Everyone began contributing examples of students who patterned undesirable behavior after others. Most of the examples were pretty grim -- kids skipping class because "everyone" cuts class, others not turning in assignments because their friends didn't have their assignments done, back talk in class because one of the leaders had a clever way of cutting teachers down.

After the discussion of the negative effects of modeling had ebbed a bit, Fran had an insight she expressed in the form of a question. "But we teachers serve as models for our students, too, don't we?"

"You bet," said Rich. "Teachers aren't merely transmitters of informa-tion about magnetic fields, past participles and the French and Indian wars. We also serve as models for students."

Skip Tennyson spoke up. "It's pretty hard for a straight, middle-class white teacher to be a model for black or Chicano students from poor back-grounds. They don't see us as models."

"Especially male students who have women teachers," said Mary, who had quit grading her papers to listen to the conversation. "How can a young black boy be influenced by anything I say? He doesn't know anything about a middle-aged white woman like me, and he doesn't want to. It's impossible to reach him."

"Don't be too sure," replied Rich. "One very recent study (Feshbach & Feshbach, 1972) investigated just that problem. The teachers were white females, and the students were all boys, some white and some black, nine to twelve years old. All 57 of the boys were shown animal pictures before the study began, and they ranked them in order of their preference. Then the group was divided into a control group of 27 and an experimental group of 30. To the experimental group the teacher made prearranged posi-tive statements about two of the animals, and negative statements about two others. For example, she said, 'Isn't that turtle nice, and so is the giraffe. But the zebra and kangaroo aren't as nice.' She made no more than two comments of this kind each day to the experimental group, and no comments at all to the control group. At the end of one week, the students again ranked the animal pictures in the order of preference, and it was found that the black boys in the experimental group changed their preferences significantly, whereas the white boys in the experi-mental group and the students in the control group showed no change. Of course, it's just one study, and it certainly doesn't answer all the ques-tions we might have, but it is an indication that despite racial differenc the teacher can influence students from other racial background, although perhaps in subtle ways."

Fran was intrigued by what Rich had said, but she thought it raised
more questions than answers. "We need to know more about all this,"
she said. "I took a psychology course that touched on observational
learning, and I remember reading then about modeling being used with
preschool kids to reduce phobias. Maybe I can find my notes. All I
remember now is that observation and imitation are important, but I
don't remember how and why they work."

While the other teachers began leaving to go home, Rich and Fran stayed
to talk together a little longer. It seemed to both of them that the
same processes that interfere with human development, such as children
imitating the wrong behavior of their friends or families, might also
be put to positive use as well. Rich said he was going to talk with
a counselor he knew and a school psychologist he had a high regard for
and see what they could suggest. Before leaving for the day, Rich and
Fran agreed they would each look into modeling, and then get together
and talk about it again.

During the next couple of weeks, the two teachers inquired into experiences of colleagues and friends concerning educational applications of
modeling. Following are some of the applications about which they
learned.

Several teachers at East High School were dismayed because the student
lunchroom was becoming extremely messy. Students were littering the
floor, leaving trays on tables, etc. The teachers recruited football
team members to help solve the problem. They and other student leaders
sat one at each table, playing the role of unofficial host. When finished,
the hosts would pick up their own trays, lunch bags, and papers along
with any others nearby and return them to bussing stations or place them
in receptacles. The hope was that other students would imitate their
behavior. While the lunchroom did not become optimally clean, a defi-
nite improvement was noted. This was attributable both to the tidiness
of the hosts and the improved clean-up habits of other students.

Madison Junior High School was using disadvantaged youngsters as lunchroom helpers. In return for their work, they received some pay as well
as lunches. However, many of these students were not work-oriented. They
were often inattentive to duty, late in reporting for work, negligent
about completing their tasks, etc. The counselors arranged to reduce the
number of such youngsters on the crew and add enough responsible, capable
others who could serve as models of more careful, thorough effort at their
tasks. By careful assignment of students to maximize modeling opportunities, and by augmenting the plan with bonuses and benefits for work well
done (an extra tip when the cashier's till balanced, for example), lunchroom staff members were able to improve the service, and the disadvantaged
youngsters acquired some useful work skills.

A counselor at Madison Junior High School became aware of a number of
students who were in serious conflict with their parents. Some of them

had left home and been returned by the police. Some were secretly living with friends, and others were contemplating running away. He set up a meeting with four of them and suggested that they study and try to practice ways of handling conflicts with parents. Then he role-played an angry parent in a typical situation, and had various students try out approaches and responses which would alleviate rather than aggravate the situation. The group continued with bi-weekly meetings. They engaged in rehearsals of ways of handling their own anger, ways of responding when falsely accused, etc. While the group meetings had not gone on long enough to permit any definitive conclusions, the counselor believed that the students' family relationships and school performance were improving.

Jack Thomas teaches special classes of emotionally disturbed youngsters at Harris Junior High School. He arranges for these students to take as many regular classes as they are capable of handling and to spend the remainder of their school day in his classroom. As they are able, he schedules them for an increasingly normal load, with the goal of returning them to a normal school day schedule. Sometimes, because of emotional outbursts to provoking situations, a student will fail in his attempt to attend regular classes. When that occurs Mr. Thomas often asks the child to role-play a number of adaptive responses to teasing or to bossiness or to criticism from a teacher, in order to prepare him to handle these situations. Mr. Thomas usually models adaptive responses prior to the role-playing.

The shop teacher at Harris Junior High School, Frank Rose, uses individualized instruction programs in his classes. After a student has performed competently a minimum set of skills, he is allowed one of several projects. The instructions for the project are on a filmstrip. Each part of the procedure is modeled on film and the student may view and study the filmstrip as many times as he wishes prior to and during completion of the project. (The filmstrips are prepared by Mr. Rose with the help of several students.

Alice Jackson attributes the alleviation of several of her teaching problems to the appearance of a good "teacher" model in the form of a school counselor. When the counselor, Penny Jones, spent an hour in Mrs. Jackson classroom helping students complete occupational interest forms and take aptitude tests, Mrs. Jackson noticed the improved rapport and responsiveness of the students. She noticed that Mrs. Jones was relaxed and pleasant, rather than tense and rigid, and that she found many things which students were doing right which she could commend. For example, she walked around the classroom as the students were working and said "Harry, that's a good idea for keeping track of your answers." When a student was making a procedural error, she called his attention to the way it should be done without embarrassing him. Mrs. Jackson later made specific use of many of the behaviors which the counselor had unwittingly modeled for her.

Fran and Rich came to several conclusions after three weeks of talking to friends and colleagues, further discussion with each other, reading, and consulting with persons who had information they needed. One was that in many instances both desirable and undesirable behavior could be attributed to observations that people make of the actions of others. Another was that there is a growing body of scientific knowledge about observational learning. Fran and Rich recognized the need to be cautious about drawing generalizations from situations that were not very similar to their own. Yet, it seemed inescapable to them that the available information was more than sufficient to justify exploration of the application of this information to life at Central High School, as well as to other places of education. To begin this exploration, Fran and Rich decided to inform their colleagues of their ideas and of the results of their inquiries. Out of this, they were sure, would come some insights into what makes the adolescent tick, and, perhaps, some practical suggestions for making life at Central more enriching for both students and faculty.

Before describing what happened when Fran and Rich sought to involve more Central faculty members in their investigation of modeling, let's look more closely at this thing called modeling. What is it? How does it work? What is known about it?

II.   WHAT IS MODELING?

The terms modeling and observational learning are often used inter-
changeably. They refer to behavior that is learned or modified as a
result of observing the behavior of others. The person whose behavior
is observed and imitated is the model.

Basic Conclusions. Following are some of the basic conclusions about
modeling reached by behavioral and learning researchers:

1. Mere observation increases the possibility of similar responses.

    For example, research has shown that some people imitate the behav-
    ior of models whom they see on television or in the movies. Some
    researchers believe readers imitate models in comic books and novels,
    too. To what extent violence on television influences the viewers
    is a matter of hot debate, but many studies show that some viewers,
    at least, are influenced.

    Everyday life provides further examples of this kind of observational
    learning. For example, when a teenager observes another successfully
    shoplifting, it increases the probability that he, too, will shoplift.
    When a student observes his friends smoking pot, he is more likely
    to smoke pot. This basic idea, of course, does not mean the observer
    necessarily will imitate the model. It simply means that seeing
    others do a specific action increases the likelihood that the obser-
    ver will do it, too. This is especially true of teen and pre-teen
    children when the model is one of their peers. One especially
    interesting real-life example occurred in an all-girl school in
    Virginia where a psychologist persuaded three high-status seniors
    to dress in a way radically different from the other girls. Within
    three weeks, 78% of the student body had imitated the dress mode of
    the three models. Every teacher and parent can testify to the
    astonishing rapidity with which a new fad of dress, hair style or
    slang will sweep through a school or neighborhood after being intro-
    duced by an admired model, be it a real life peer leader or a fantasy
    hero on film.

2. What happens to the model influences the observer.

    a. Reinforcement. If the model is reinforced or rewarded, the
        observer is more likely to imitate the model's behavior. Rein-
        forcement refers to any event (stimulus) which, if contingent
        upon a response made by an individual, increases the probability
        or likelihood that that response will be repeated. Praise from
        a teacher is frequently a highly reinforcing event.

        An important factor is whether or not the person who is being
        observed is positively reinforced or rewarded for behaving in

a particular manner. One tends to imitate responses that pay
off. Wittingly or not, teachers influence many of the consequences of their pupil's behavior. They give grades and check-
marks, they smile and frown, praise and criticize, ignore and
reward. By providing certain kinds of consequences, teachers
influence their pupil's behavior. They can increase the occurrence of desired behaviors and decrease the occurrence of those
which are not desirable. One of the possibilities open to
teachers is positive reinforcement (smiles, verbal approval) for
modeling by children that is adaptive and in a developmental
direction. Punishment (a scolding, criticism) can be applied
in cases of undesirable modeling -- for example, when peer pressure pushes children to imitate their peers in picking on other
classmates. Sarason, Glaser, and Fargo (1972) have written a
pamphlet, Reinforcing Productive Classroom Behavior, especially
for teachers interested in learning about reinforcement and
other techniques useful in modifying pupils' behavior.

Many research studies have demonstrated the positive influence
on other students when one student (a model) is rewarded for his
good performance or behavior. (Woody, 1969) Everyday life examples of this abound. Every teacher can tell of instances of a
smart-talking student who gets laughs from the others for his
remarks and is soon imitated by other students. The student
who cheats and gets away with it may encourage a rash of cheating
on the part of other students. In a more positive vein, verbal
praise for winning a spelling match encourages some other students to try and receive the same praise.

Like all other forms of human behavior, however, reinforcement
is complex. The motivation of some students, as all teachers
know, may not be heightened when one of their peers succeeds and
receives rewards. In general, however, rewards for achievement
do influence the students who observe the model receive reward,
for better or for worse. The teacher who knows of this effect
can better handle each situation as it arises to maximize its
influence on all of the students who are observing.

b. Punishment. If the model is punished, the observer is less
likely to imitate the model's behavior.

Again, every teacher will think of examples. One real-life situation involved a high school where a group of Chicanos who spoke
poor English were being hassled by a group of high-prestige
students. The principal issued a firm and clear warning about
what would happen if it continued. When the behavior did continue, the high-prestige group was reprimanded in public, made
to apologize, and had privileges withdrawn. There was no more
trouble. In the cheating example above, if the cheating model
is found out and suffers the consequences of his cheating,

observing students are much less likely to turn to cheating themselves. However, as with all the general principles laid down, common sense must be applied; an outrageous punishment can create a backlash from the observing students by creating sympathy for the offender.

c. Unknown Outcome. If the observer does not know what happens to the model, the effect of reward or punishment is reduced.

When teachers employ reward or punishment as an additional tool to facilitate observational learning, it is important that the observing students know definitely what are the consequences for the model. For example, one school showed a film on stolen cars which concluded with the teenage culprits being sentenced to reform school. However, when the audience was asked what had happened, many of them thought the thieves had been let off and sent to boarding school.

3. What happens to the observer influences his behavior.

Studies of behavior show the importance of whether the observer is rewarded or punished after having made an imitative response. The youngster whose warm relationship with his teacher leads him to emulate the teacher's behavior in the classroom may be punished for this behavior on the playground. His peers may poke fun at him for being teacher's pet. A realistic account of behavior in the school and elsewhere requires recognition of its social context and the fact that classroom behavior is influenced by many, often conflicting, forces.

4. Behavior rehearsal.

When modeling is effective, behavior is observed and then copied by the onlookers. Behavioral rehearsal further encourages the modeled response. This is done by giving the observer a chance to role-play the response after he has observed the model until it becomes a familiar part of his repertory.

One simple example of this is Francie, a girl who never talked in class. She never asked questions, never made comments. Two of her friends felt sorry for her, and with the help of a school counselor, they arranged modeling and role-playing sessions. The girls pretended they were in the classroom, and the two more assertive girls demonstrated for Francie how they asked questions, even mentioned that they were nervous before speaking out. Then they told Francie what to say while one of them played the role of teacher. Gradually Francie was able, albeit timidly, to address questions and comments to "teacher." After a few days of this behavior rehearsal Francie actually raised her hand and asked the real teacher a question.

In a more elaborate example the youngster was an extremely withdrawn boy. He would neither look at nor talk to other students. For two weeks a therapist observed and measured the boy's behavior and that of other students as to touching, looking at others, being in close proximity to others, talking, and playing or working with others. These measures were obtained to establish a baseline of interpersonal behavior for the withdrawn boy. Then a male psychology student served as a model, and over a period of seven weeks he first established a system of rewards for any imitative behavior the boy exhibited. Before long the youngster was imitating the model in several small ways. Once this pattern was established, the model began joining the group of other children. At first the boy wouldn't even watch, so the therapist provided a running commentary on his activities, including his reluctance to join the other children. Bit by bit, the withdrawn boy began to follow the lead of the model until at the end of seven weeks he was able to interact socially with the others in the classroom. Although this example is too lengthy and time-consuming for most classroom situations, it does provide an interesting explanation of how modeling can be applied to even serious problems.

A familiar illustration of another variety of modeled behavior is the Dateline column in many newspapers. It contains advice for teenagers written by Ele and Walt Dulaney. In their column the Dulaneys give word-for-word examples to those who write in concerning what to say to a girl friend who smokes too much, what to say to friends who don't know about a family tragedy, and step-by-step ways to handle situations the inquirers feel are too tough for the average teenager to deal with.

5. The model himself.

Anybody might be a model for a child -- a parent, teacher, sibling, friend, or TV character. Both research and common experience indicate that the observer will imitate the model's behavior more readily if he admires, respects, or for some other reason wants to imitate the model. Peer models are perhaps the most imitated. Everyone is familiar with Alcoholics Anonymous, Synanon, Mental Patients Anonymous, and similar groups. These illustrate people who have actually experienced the problem of alcohol or drugs or mental illness and they seem to be more successful than are the professionals in modifying the behavior of others with similar problems.

One real-life example occurred in a California elementary school composed largely of disadvantaged youngsters. The principal hired a clean-cut, upper middle-class university student to start a noon-hour athletic program. The young man didn't look, act or talk like anyone the children knew, and the program failed. Later the principal hired a tough, badly-dressed college boy who spoke broken English complete with ghetto slang, and was a fine athlete. The second model turned out to be highly effective.

Effective models can come from a background different from that of
the observers if the students perceive the model as someone they
want to emulate. Furthermore, one person may be an effective model
for some students but not for others. Each situation has to be
evaluated on its own terms.

A word might also be said about ineffective models. Teachers may
unwittingly act in ways that interfere with the student's desire
to emulate them. Students are less likely to identify and imitate
teachers who appear to the students to be overly concerned about
matters that are either irrelevant, relatively unimportant, or
unreal to them (for example, chewing gum, wearing tennis shoes,
using "in" colloquialisms). A teacher's inordinate ridicule, con-
tempt, or disrespect for actions of the students could similarly
have a negative effect ("Why would you want to read that magazine?").

While it may be elusive, the relationship between the observer and
the model is an important variable in observational learning. The
relationship may be quite real in the sense that it was fostered
by considerable social interaction, or it might be on a fantasy
or symbolic level. Even when a modeled response is definitely
useful to an observer, he may not adopt it if he is not attracted
to the model. Some teachers are especially effective in their
teaching because they create relationships with their pupils that
make it relatively easy and comfortable for the pupils to accept
criticisms of their work and corrections of their mistakes. The
teacher who is able to admit and matter-of-factly accept his own
errors can be a good model for his pupils. For example, one high
school social studies teacher who was both competent and experienced became increasingly annoyed one day at the tangential and
close to impertinent questions asked by a few of his students.
After answering the questions, the teacher returned to his material
but found he had lost his place in his notes. As he struggled to
remember what he wished to convey, his class soon filled with
laughter at his confusion. Having enough objectivity to see the
humor in his predicament, he joined the class in laughing at his
plight. Then he turned to the impertinent questioners, pointed
his finger at them, and with a smile on his face said: "You got
me this time -- but just you wait!" The teacher felt that this
good-natured display of his own weakness seemed to draw him and his
pupils together. Interestingly there was a reduction in unproductive
questions after the incident.

Writers who stress the cognitive (thinking) aspects of modeling often
refer to identification, an important developmental process. The
term identification refers to the presence of an emotional tie
causing a person to think, feel, and act as he imagines the person
does with whom he has the tie. It might be said that whereas imitation
refers to a person's reproduction of a specific response made by a

model, identification connotes a more general process whereby a model comes to be like a significant person in an observer's life. This process of "coming to be like" may be much more complex than the simple imitation of particular aspects of a model's behavior. It involves, in addition, an emotional relationship between two persons.

The role of identification seems particularly apparent in such developmental processes as conformity to social norms. Children do not just naturally conform to standards set for them. They frequently take on as their own the standards, values, and attitudes of the persons with whom they identify. Identification may involve both selectivity and ambivalence. Selectivity in identification may be observed when a child is like one parent in some respects and like the other parent in other respects. The child does not indiscriminately imitate all responses made by all potential models. Ambivalence in identification may be observed when he reaches the point in development at which he can respond cognitively to the identifications that he has formed. Everyone has probably had contact with persons who have in particular instances made remarks such as, "It's too bad I take after my mother." This would suggest that although a girl may in some ways become like her mother, she may also have significant negative emotional and cognitive reactions to certain acquired behaviors in her repertory. Even girls who declare that they will bring up their children very differently from the way they were raised discover at times that they are repeating their parent's behavior.

Because it may be difficult to describe the relationship between the model and the observer, some writers have advocated limiting usage of the terms modeling and observational learning to the copying by the observer of observable responses. But the relationship between the model and the observer (which it may not be possible to describe entirely in terms of observable events) can influence the observer's thinking processes as well as his overt behavior. For example, it may be necessary that the acquisition of skills for novel and creative thinking be preceded by acquisition of the ability to explore unlikely paths to solutions. The teacher who provides students with examples of this form of adventurousness may help them develop that unique orientation often necessary for creative thought.

The model does not have to be a paragon. He should be someone credible to the observer and with whom the latter can identify. A classmate -- and not necessarily the top performer -- might be an effective model for some students. The best student may be seen by the observer as representing an impossibly high standard to attain, and this could result in the rejection of the model. Perhaps a distinction can be drawn between a model who displays credible coping behavior and the perfect exemplary model. The coping model is someone with whom the observer can identify and who may even display some responses that the observer sees in himself and doesn't admire. A student

who has no discernible academic motivation may benefit much more
from contact with a formerly uninvolved (academically) student who
has made a few strides towards active participation in school life
than with the exemplary straight-A student who is headed for college.
Scientific knowledge about observational learning and the model's
characteristics is incomplete. However, it is clear that the
credibility of the model and his actual or symbolic link with the
learner may be crucial.

6. The possible response.

The foregoing seemingly self-evident idea is easy to overlook, especially in the crowded classroom most teachers must handle. For
example, a student with minimal brain dysfunction may be completely
incapable of sitting still in his seat and one with an uncorrected
sight problem cannot properly do his work. Other educational tools
must be employed to determine what a student can and cannot do,
and the teacher must set goals for each student that are high enough,
yet at the same time are not too high. This is one of the times
when the art rather than the science of teaching becomes important.

Adaptive and Nonadaptive Behavior

Clinical workers have gathered much evidence supporting the notion that
observational learning plays a part in the acquisition of a variety of
undesirable response patterns. For example, the intense self-preoccupying
fears of a child or adult may represent an exaggeration of a major or minor
fear displayed by a parent. The mother who persistently checks to see
if the door is locked may be copied by her observant child. Television,
the perennial companion of our children today, presents a symbolic modeling experience for observers. There may be significant links between
the mass media, including television, and certain types of undesirable
behavior, such as aggression or fear. Commercials notwithstanding,
television is not a systematically programmed technique for influencing
people, and consequently, controlled studies of televised modeling experiences can contribute to understanding its effects.

But undesirable responses are not the only ones acquired through observation. Necessary or desirable social, vocational and educational skills
are also learned through modeling. A familiar example is the apprentice-
ship period in the skilled trades during which the apprentice learns
the work behavior of the journeyman.

Another positive example concerns George, the leader of a neighborhood
gang that had been stealing and mugging. When he announced to his group
that he had taken a part-time job, three members of the gang also applied
for jobs. Although none of the gang had heard of modeling, George's
decision to work for spending money rather than to steal it influenced
the behavior of his friends.

One teacher recounted the following example of a naturalistic modeling situation. He was supervising several adolescent boys on a paid work experience project. One task involved shoveling a large pile of peat-moss onto a truck for transport to a site being landscaped. The teacher began to shovel the bark with a smooth, long-stroked scooping motion while the boys struggled with the unwieldly material in several less adaptive ways. The teacher presently noticed one of the boys observing his shoveling technique. The boy immediately began to imitate the scooping motion, and within a few minutes the other boys were copying this more effective method. Interestingly, no verbal communication occurred during this sequence of modeling, observation and imitation.

Modeling and Reinforcement

Why is it that modeling experiences may lead to noticeable and sometimes dramatic changes in behavior? Perhaps the main reason is that these experiences provide the individual with information. Whether a particular imitative response is acquired after only one observational opportunity (this might be termed no-trial learning) or more gradually, each of us can think of many examples of modeling.

However, the fact that observational learning is so common should not mislead us into believing that it necessarily occurs as a result of a simple process. Johnny may behave like his father in many ways but the causes of the similarities may vary widely. A person may incorporate a model's responses into his own repertory on the basis of observation alone, but reinforcement or reward for making an imitative response may increase the probability of emission of the modeled behavior.

III. HOW MODELING WORKS

"Why Should I Buy That Package?"

Reading, talking and thinking about modeling had been stimulating for
Fran and Rich. They were now aware that a large amount of research had
been carried out on modeling and the conditions conducive to imitation.
They felt also that other faculty members at Central would -- or, at
least, should -- be interested in what they had turned up. How should
they use their new found knowledge? Rich noted that within a week there
would be a faculty meeting. Although most of these meetings were taken
up primarily with "business" -- announcements, reports, and appointments
of committees -- occasionally, there was a void of 20 minutes that was
filled by a faculty member with something on his mind.

A check of the agenda for the meeting seemed to provide Fran and Rich
with their opportunity. It was enhanced by a committee report presented
just before they went on. The committee was part of a city-wide effort
to determine the extent and causes of the lack of academic achievement
and dropping out among high school students. The committee chairman made
two points that shocked many of those who were in attendance at the
meeting. Compared to the national achievement test norms, Central stood
in the bottom 30 percent. A few teachers commented that this low level
of performance was due in large measure to low motivation among the
students. The other shocker was the dropout rate, reported by the committee to be over 35 percent. Skip Tennyson commented that what the
faculty at Central needed was not more knowledge in their respective
fields, but a better feel for the adolescent -- especially the disadvantaged one -- and an understanding of how to reach and form a genuine
human relationship with him.

If anything, Skip's comment seemed to deepen the pall cast over the group
by the committee report. It certainly put an end to discussion. Everyone wanted to avoid adding to the thickness of the atmosphere, and no
one had anything cheerful to say. In this atmosphere Mr. Penney, the
principal, said that Fran and Rich wanted to make an informal report
on some ideas that they had put together.

Fran and Rich had decided earlier that Rich should make the presentation.
He had been at Central for 12 years -- 10 years longer than Fran -- and
knew personally many more faculty members than she did. They also had
agreed that they would talk about observational learning in a very low-
key way, emphasizing that most of the information about modeling had come
from research in settings other than the classroom. As he talked Rich
did not put emphasis on modeling as a cure-all nor as a simple and direct
way of cutting the dropout problem but rather, presented it as an idea
that might be worth exploring further. He explained that the students
at Central were exposed to many models differing in their attractiveness,

their ability to perform different tasks, and their skill at influencing others. The main point made by Rich during his 15-minute talk was the fact that modeling is a process of social influence. While there are gaping holes in present-day knowledge, he concluded, perhaps a few of us would like to pursue further the question of social influence and the notion of modeling in particular.

Mr. Penney was more than supportive, complimenting Rich and Fran for their scholarship and willingness to share their ideas with colleagues. A few of their colleagues also threw verbal bouquets at the two teachers. Then Mary Clay stood up and said she appreciated all the work that had gone into Rich and Fran's presentation, and she understood the importance developmentally of having good models with whom children could identify, but what about high-school-age kids who may have had a long history of undesirable experiences and exposures to inadequate or even harmful models? Mary could see that exposure to good models helps make for good adjustment. But does anyone really know whether good models are helpful in overcoming behavior problems and the effects of poverty, lack of stimulation, and perhaps even neglect? "Why should I buy your package? Does modeling work?", she asked.

Fran started to stand up, but before she could say anything, Bill Bennett, one of the counselors, spoke up. He wondered if Rich and Fran might not find it worthwhile relating their work on modeling to something he had been interested in for a long time, role-playing. He said that role-playing was a therapeutic technique which requires an individual to try out new roles other than his own. Role-playing permits a more objective observation of the details and subtleties of social roles than might be gained through verbal description alone. "Aren't models important influences over role-playing?" Bill asked. He looked as though he had an answer to that question himself, but before he could present it to the group, Jim Penney, the principal, pointed out that the clock on the wall said 5:02 and that the 5 o'clock adjournment rule should be adhered to. However, he commented that the notion of modeling was obviously a provocative one. "Would those faculty members interested in pursuing it further be willing to sit together in the lunch room tomorrow in order to talk things over?" Fran's and Rich's hands went up, and so did five others. Thus was founded what Jim Penney dubbed the Central GAM -- the Central Group for the Advancement of Modeling.

Modeling To Change Undesirable Behavior

At the first meeting of Central GAM, Rich pointed out that much of the work on modeling has had to do with fears and how to reduce or eliminate them -- things like little children who are scared of dogs and adults who are terrified of snakes.

Snakes. "Let me read to you an introduction to a modeling program used by one psychologist, P. K. Carlson, to help college students who were intensely afraid of snakes."

One of the ways we can tell that a person is afraid of something is by the way he behaves in its presence. For example, we infer that you are afraid of snakes because you have refused to handle one. If you could learn to handle snakes then we would no longer have a basis for saying that you were afraid of them. One of the best ways to learn a new behavior is to watch someone else perform it first and then try to imitate their performance. Psychologists have already used this technique successfully in a wide variety of situations. It is the technique that we will use here to teach you to handle snakes without fear. What will happen is this: each time that we meet I will demonstrate a behavior with a snake, then you in turn will be asked to imitate my behavior. When you have successfully done so we will move on to another somewhat more difficult behavior. By the time we are finished you should be able to comfortably handle snakes (Carlson, 1969, p. 20).

Rich then explained that what Carlson had done was to approach, touch, and handle a three-foot boa constrictor while the fearful students looked on. The students were encouraged to copy what Carlson did with the snake. He found that this approach was highly effective. The students' first approach responses to the snake were, of course, highly tentative, but the combination of the opportunity to observe a fearless model and to practice handling the snake fearlessly themselves made them significantly more confident that they were, eliminating what had heretofore been for them a nagging, even terrifying concern.

Dogs. A similar approach has been followed with 4-and 5-year-old children who were afraid of dogs. Whereas the model in the Carlson study was Carlson himself, the models in several studies of fearful preschoolers have been peers, preschoolers who in an unfearful manner played with dogs. After observing these peer models, a significant number of 4-and 5-year-olds were able to relinquish their fears and actually to enjoy playing with dogs. A growing number of controlled experiments show that a model who demonstrates mastery or lack of fear over a situation has a positive effect on persons who experience fear in that direction.

Tests. These encouraging results have led researchers, educators, and counselors to expand the domain for which modeling might be helpful. One area that has been explored is test anxiety -- that is, fear and self-preoccupation in situations in which the student is aware that his performance is being evaluated. Each of us probably has personal knowledge of cases in which students have done poorly on tests and in class because of worry over what the teacher or parents or other students will think of their work. Exposure to models who demonstrate efficient and work-manlike approaches to tests has been found to reduce test anxiety in the fearful student.

Chain of behavior. Psychological research has shown that the modeled behavior should include not only the terminal response (running the race, taking the test, playing with the dog) but also responses that occur earlier in the chain of behavior. For example, before he can take important examinations confidently, the highly test-anxious student needs training in focusing his full attention on tests while working on them. For this purpose, it might be better for the model to display the gradual acquisition of the desired behavior rather than perfect performance from the outset. (Observing the behavior of a crack miler as he runs that distance in 3:58 minutes will not by itself enable us to copy his behavior.) A fearful student who is too self-preoccupied may need to learn how to attend to the task at hand more completely before he comes to grips with the terminal behavior, for example, taking a test.

Assertive Training

One reason why observing the final product (the 3:58 mile, the exemplary oral book report) may not be enough is that individuals with the same problems may have acquired them in different ways. Take the well-motivated student who, because of timidity and fear of embarrassment, is unable to bring himself to ask questions of his teacher. In several subjects (mathematics, for example) it is hazardous to go on to the next step until there is a clear understanding of preceding steps. The student who cannot ask questions at the optimal time (that is, when he first experiences puzzlement) is at a considerable handicap. His problem is primarily the inability to be assertive in a situation where assertiveness (putting up his hand and asking his question) is not only desirable but also necessary to understanding.

Assertive training is an important type of modeling. It is especially helpful in encouraging desirable responses rather than in suppressing undesirable ones. The first step in assertive training is the identification of the behavior deficit. Following this, the individual is given demonstrations by a model of how to emit the behavior that presently occurs too infrequently. Finally, the individual engages in behavioral rehearsal, which consists of his practicing, through role-playing, the modeled behavior. Francie, the shy girl mentioned earlier who couldn't ask questions in class, was a most appropriate candidate for and did receive assertive training.

The teacher who shows that he likes pupils' questions, even those that seem "dumb," helps create an environment in which appropriate assertive responses can develop. Although asking questions is but one component of adaptive behavior in the classroom, its importance should not be underestimated. Another component is students' relationships with one another. The unassertive student who is too compliant, too easily pushed around by his peers may pay both an academic and a personal price for his inability to stand up to others. For example, he may be unable to say "no" to the classmate who wants to borrow his class notes even though he needs them himself. The following excerpt from a taped training program was developed by two psychologists to stiffen the backbones of college students who are deficient in assertiveness.

Narrator: A person in one of your classes, someone whom you do not know very well, borrowed your class notes weeks ago, then failed to return them at the next class, thus forcing you to take notes on scrap paper. Now this person comes up to you again and says, "Hey, mind if I borrow your class notes again?" What do you say? (Subject practices responding, either overtly or covertly).

Narrator: Now, listen to the responses of two assertive subjects to this same situation.

Male Model: You didn't return my notes last time, so I'm not going to lend them to you this time.

Female Model: No, I just can't be sure you're going to have them back in time.

Narrator: (Coaching) Notice that both of these assertive subjects let the person know that their refusal was based on his past behavior. Their responses were brief and without any ambiguity. Their voices expressed some irritation over the past behavior of this person, but in general their responses were well controlled. Now, (listen to/ think back to) your response to this situation and compare it to the response of the models you have just heard. (Playback or 10-second pause).

Narrator: Now you will hear the same situation again. This time try to make your response more assertive. (Repeat situation. Subject practices responding). (McFall & Lillesand, 1971).

In this example of assertive training there are two important components: (1) the students are exposed to models and (2) the students engage in behavioral rehearsal. The second point relates to role-playing. In this case it was a step toward seeing themselves as persons who could say "No" when there was adequate justification for noncompliance. The person who observes appropriate assertive behavior in others, practices it himself, and is perhaps rewarded (for example, through praise) for his first rudimentary assertive responses may begin to think of himself in more positive terms. He may become more confident and expressive in a variety of situations that seem only tangentially related to the modeling opportunities that were afforded.

Modeling often has been employed with normal people whose problems may be distressing but are not seriously disabling (fearful preschoolers, students worried about tests). It has also been used with markedly deviant and disturbed groups -- for example, prisoners and schizophrenic patients. In one experiment with prisoners between the ages of 18 and 20 (Stumphauzer, 1972), the inmates were given the opportunity to observe older, prestigious peer models choose between things they could have immediately (for example, a small amount of money) or a more valuable reward for which there would be a delay. The prisoners whose models chose the

-18-

delayed rewards themselves later chose the more valuable delayed rewards more often than did prisoners who did not observe a model. This experimental demonstration is of suggestive value because so many crimes are commiteed by persons who are deficient in planning for the future and whose susceptibility to present temptations is too strong. This is, of course, relevant to the domain of education because many students who cut classes, drop out, and behave in a delinquent manner have poorly developed concepts of the future. They often have little awareness of the need occasionally to pass up immediate gains in order to lay the groundwork for more substantial ones in the future.

* * * *

After Rich and Fran had completed this review of their notes and what they could remember from their reading and discussions with knowledgeable people, Mary Clay said admiringly, "Well, I guess you guys did your homework. What paragon did you have as a model?"

Bill Bennett, the school counselor who had mentioned the possible connection between modeling and role-playing, took on the role of the assertive leader at this point. "We've come a long way since that faculty meeting yesterday. Rich and Fran have reeled off a long list of studies that show us that their enthusiasm about modeling is well founded. It would be nice if they could give us some recipes to solve neatly the problems of the kids who are giving us our current headaches."

After a moment of reflection Bill went on, "In a way, maybe we have to learn to be patient and work toward long-term goals just as did those prisoners. I think we're now at the point where we've gotten hold of some valuable principles of behavior. Applying them to our own situations is up to us."

Mary Clay, yesterday's skeptic, got in the last word. "I don't think we should drop this modeling thing. Yesterday we heard about some new ideas. Today, Rich and Fran backed up those ideas with research evidence. I suggest that each of us think about the idea of modeling from the point of view of our situation and see if anything productive emerges. Let's meet at lunch again on Friday."

Everybody agreed with Mary's conclusion and the back-to-class march began again. As they were walking down the hall, Bill Bennett mentioned to Mary that he was going to look into modeling not only as it relates to the classroom but to the school counseling situation as well.

Dropouts & Peer Leaders

Bill came on strong at the next GAM meeting. He had been talking to a counselor friend at East Side High who had a few good ideas and this counselor in turn referred him to someone in the state Department of

Education who was especially interested in vocational education. The state man had given Bill a few statistics that were eye-openers and not very pleasing. About 30 percent of all high school students in the United States do not graduate from high school (that's 15 million of the 50 million students). This staggering number of dropouts enter the labor market essentially unprepared. About 40 million students who start college will not complete it, and only 6 million will have had any significant amount of vocational education. For millions of students, what they are learning in schools is probably not so much "wrong" as basically inappropriate. In one careful study of 440,000 high school students across the country, it was found that the schools fail to help students develop a sense of personal responsibility for their own educational, personal, and social development (Flanagan, 1967). Bill told his colleagues that the schools needed to do more work in what he called psychological education. "Traditional academic education, of course, must continually be strengthened and upgraded, but kids have to know what to do with it, and they have to be motivated to pursue it."

Then Bill made an observation that struck a responsive chord in his fellow faculty members. "As I think back on the failures, the dropouts, and other school problem cases I've seen and heard about, I'm impressed with the fact that a high percentage of them are not particuarly dramatic. We hear a lot about delinquents and troublemakers, but what about those millions of dropouts and poor performers who are quiet and unresponsive, who just seem to disappear from view? We often don't make contact with those kids, and because of more pressing problems, we neglect them.

"I want to tell you about a study the state man told me about. It was carried out in Detroit. The participants were 11th grade students who were predominantly black and who came from lower socioeconomic backgrounds (Vriend, 1969). A high percentage of these students could be described as underachievers, passive learners, and dropout-prone.

"Each student in the experimental program participated in special group meetings once a week during the school year. A school counselor led each session. But the real leaders were kids who had experienced school success and possessed interpersonal skills which it was felt would help low-performing students to become more achievement oriented. The peer leaders, of course, had to be trained, and they were encouraged to use faculty members as resource persons as the need arose."

Bill passed around typed copies of parts of a tape recorded session.

Jack: Let's talk about from slave to master.

Bob: We talked about prejudice and race last time.

Jack: I don't mean that! Who knows what I mean?

Vinnie: (A peer leader) Go ahead and tell us because you may mean anything.

Carl: (Another peer leader) Yeah!

Jack: Well, like the other day when I made a smart remark, Mrs.
         Smith said that if I wasn't careful, I'd find my head and
         learn to think. Well, I call that from slave to master
         because when you think better than the other dude you've
         become the master and I like being the master!

Victor: Right on. Everytime I get in trouble it's because I didn't
         think about something first.

Al: I know you're always in trouble but I don't know what you're
         saying now.

Victor: Well, you know, like in a class or something, when you say
         something that makes the teacher mad or start an argument with
         another dude.

Carl: Or like we was talking about the other day -- if you're out
         messing around the other dudes start drinking or something.
         If you didn't think ahead of time what to do, you might just
         go along and end up getting busted.

Javk: Well, I guess that's part of it too, but I was thinking about
         what you learn -- like when you read and you kind of fight
         in your head to figure out what the man says.

Frank: No way! I just want answers to the questions, man. I don't
         care whether I believe them or not.

Jack: But look, man, that's why I like debating because you learn
         facts and use them. You can take the same facts and use them
         in different ways to wipe out the other dudes.

Frank: What good is that after the debate?

Jack: Those facts are in my head. Right here. (Points to head) I
         know them and that makes me strong. Nobody can change that!

Counselor: Jack, are you saying then, that the ability to use ideas
            is a kind of power in itself, and that what you learn is never
            wasted!

Randy: Man, there's enough to study without messing up your head with
         stuff you don't need.

Vinnie: (A peer leader) But you need to learn more. Like, if a class
         is a drag but you make yourself think then it's not such a
         drag because you've got something to do, man.

After they had read the two mimeographed sheets, there were a number of reactions. Fran was impressed with the fact that frequently peer leaders could say things in a way that a member of the staff (teacher, counselor) could not.

John Reddin, a mathematics teacher, said that groups which included peer leaders could be especially effective because they provided less able and adept students with believable examples they could emulate.

Rich wondered what would happen if such an experiment were carried out at Central. He felt that some procedure involving student and teacher nominations could be worked out to select the peer leaders. Fran raised the question of when such a group would meet, she then decided that if the program really was worth instituting, she was sure something could be worked out -- for example, meeting during study periods, or perhaps as part of social studies, or maybe after school as an extracurricular activity. Rich pointed out that there probably would be no problem in selecting student participants since there were plenty of problem students at Central. Bill Bennett wasn't so sure about the selection issue. He wondered if the quiet kids who couldn't bring themselves to ask the teacher questions would become more withdrawn if placed with the behavioral problem and overly aggressive kids.

Mary, the skeptic, said she wanted to find out if there was any objective evidence that the peer counseling approach worked. Could Bill Bennett help her out on this point?

Bill said that students in the Detroit study of groups with peer leaders had been compared in several ways with similar students not given special group experience. Several before-and-after comparisons were made. These indicated that the youngsters in the experimental program showed significant gains in reading, social studies, and in the area of verbal expression. However, the experimental and control groups had not differed either before or after the special program in mathematics or ability to handle quantitative concepts. In general, the peer counseling groups showed significantly more improvement in overall course grades than did the control group.

Bill went on to point out that students who had participated in the special program experienced heightened levels of vocational aspirations. Equally important, they became more confident of attaining their goals. The control group had actually shown decreases in both areas -- aspirations and expectations.

Bill mentioned a few other findings. The peer counseling group showed improvement in attendance and punctuality, while the control group showed declines. When the experimental students themselves were asked to evaluate the program they were highly enthusiastic, saying that they had profited from observing others and that they had been able to say and do things in the sessions that represented steps forward. Bill's conclusion was that peer leaders could be quite effective in a lower-class school if special efforts were made to provide teacher support and perhaps rewards for improved academic behavior. He felt it important to note that the achieving peer leaders who had served as such effective helpers in the experiment he had described all had come from disadvantaged backgrounds.

Harriet Schultz then put in her two cents worth prefacing it by saying that somehow the GAM's discussions and Rich's and Bill's reports had encouraged her to state publicly some opinions she had held for a long time. Harriet, a social studies teacher, had a reputation as a fair, intelligent, well-read, but rather shy person. She said that the application of the peer modeling idea to the classroom setting did not really involve any new principles. She mentioned that several books she recently had read described the wide use of peer groups and peer leaders in educational and social programs in other countries as well as in the United States. She believed also that the faster the artificial distinctions between educational, social, and vocational development are done away with, the better.

While a counselor had been involved in each of the peer leader groups in the study they had just discussed, Harriet believed that teachers might have been equally effective. She pointed out that the study was not a perfect one. For example, the same positive results might have been obtained if the counselor had not been present and the peer leaders had been completely on their own. In fact, Harriet said, she really liked the idea of the students' running their own group, with the help of specially invited consultants, like teachers, counselors, and administrators. "I guess what we have heard today is a model of educational experimentation -- that's a mouthful, isn't it? We can copy the peer modeling project, but maybe each school with its own peculiar problems has to carry out its own experiments. We should build on the knowledge gained by others -- and profit by their mistakes, too -- but I think we should be daring enough to plot our own course."

Not everyone concurred with Harriet but they all agreed that there were a number of ways in which the social learning process at Central could be greatly improved. As the bell sounded, Harriet, who more and more looked like a graduate of a course on assertive modeling, insisted on sharing one of her favorite quotations with her colleagues. It was something that the sociologist Emile Durkheim had once said: "Education is only the image and reflection of society."

IV. APPLYING WHAT HAS BEEN LEARNED ABOUT MODELING TO DELINQUENTS

"Let's Write Some Scripts of our Own . . ."

At the next meeting, Bill had more handouts for his colleagues. They
came from a project that had been conducted at Cascadia Juvenile Reception-
Diagnostic Center in Tacoma, Washington, an institution for juvenile delinquents. The youngsters there had already done many of the things
Central faculty members were afraid their students might do. The idea
behind the Cascadia project was similar to the one that stimulated the
peer counseling method: observation and imitation of adaptive behavior.
The Cascadia work differed, however, in that it was somewhat more tightly
structured and organized. The delinquents, boys between the ages of 15
and 18, observed models enact specific problems and their solutions. The
boys then had to imitate as faithfully as they could the behavior that
had been modeled for them. The emphasis, accordingly, was not on talking
about specific topics but simply on copying modeled behavior.

Bill pointed out that what this amounted to was a combination of the
boys' observation of modeled behavior and then participation in well-
structured role imitations similar to behavioral rehearsal. After the
boys had taken their turns at role-playing, the models, who were psychology
graduate students, would make a few brief discussion points, answer questions, and then adjourn the meeting.

This was one of the scripts in the material Bill distributed.

Cutting Class

Introduction. Most guys seem to agree that finishing school is a good
idea. Almost everyone figures he'll get a high school diploma someday.
However, some guys think that graduating is too far in the future to worry
about now. They don't study, cut school a lot, and end up out of school
and in trouble. Going back to school after having been in trouble is
also pretty hard. Most guys on parole want to finish high school but
most of them also have problems doing it. The scene today is about one
of these problems. After the scene we will talk about the problem presented and other problems that you guys might have with school.

Scene: At school during lunch. Joe and George are sitting next to each
other at a table.

Joe: Hey, George, it's a really great day. Let's take off this after-
         noon and go to the beach. It'll sure beat getting trapped in that
         crummy hot classroom all afternoon.

George: Swimming would be great. I'd like to go, but, look man, the
         water will still be there after school. Let's go then.

-24-

Joe: After school? After the sun sets? What's the matter, have you got the hots for Miss Carlson? You used to cut school all the time.

George: No more...I'm on parole. I've got to stay in school if I don't want to get sent up again.

Joe: What's skipping one afternoon gonna hurt? Your parole counselor will never know the difference.

George: Yeah, but if I cut with you today, I'll bet I'll be the guy you'll look up the next time you want to cut out for the beach. If I get on that, pretty soon I'd hardly be going to school at all any more.

Joe: So what? I skip a lot and it doesn't bother me.

George: That's your business. I got into trouble in the first place 'cuz I was skipping school a lot and fooling around. You guys go ahead. I don't want to run the risk of getting kicked out of school. Man, I want to graduate and the time to worry about doing it is right now.

Joe: Yeah, look why don't you come on along this once.

George: Yeah, and I want to go along, but later, not now. How about getting together at three?

Joe: That's a lot of wasted sun. I'll see if Pete will go with me. If he does, we'll head out now and we'll look for you at the beach at three. If he won't either, let's meet at the car at three. Okay?

George: Okay.

Discussion points. 1. Ability to resist temptation. 2. Special school problems of parolee. 3. Importance of finishing school. 4. Reasons for skipping school and their validity. 5. "Vicious circle" aspects -- skipping carries with it the chance of getting caught which leads to further avoidance of school (truancy) to avoid punishment. (Sarason & Ganzer, 1971, pp. 122-123).

Rich observed that the idea behind the script seemed similar to a research study they had discussed at an earlier meeting. "In that study, the aim was to get the subjects, who were prisoners, to give up immediate rewards for more significant delayed ones. In this script, the boy who was being tempted to cut class modeled resistance to temptation."

"One thing I like about the script," said Fran, "was that George, the tempted boy, seemed pretty confident in pursuing the path that he wanted to follow."

In anticipation of the usual Mary Clay question, Bill said, "Okay, but what were the results?" He went on, "The researchers discovered that the combination of modeling and role-playing resulted in much better adjustment within the institution -- for example, fewer discipline problems, better social relationships. Even more important, they found that when they were back in their communities, two to three years after they had been in the modeling groups, the recidivism rate was half that found among control subjects."

Mary interrupted, "What is the recidivism rate?"

"That's the rate of repeat crimes -- a criminal who is jailed and then released becomes a recidivist when he commits another crime."

Bill went on, "One other thing. There was another group in the Cascadia study that didn't have the modeling but did participate in guided discussion groups that dealt with exactly the same material covered in the modeling scenes. The discussions were structured and not freewheeling talkathons. The aim was to provide the boys with information about how the world worked and the role they could play in it. The researchers obtained good results with this technique too."

Rich had a question, "The scene in which George refused to cut class had to do with resisting temptations. What were some of the other scripts that were used in the Cascadia research?"

Bill answered, "Some of the scripts presented ways of coping with authority figures so as to stand up for your rights without making an enemy of someone you like and with whom you work. Other scenes dealt with how to present yourself at a job interview, how to avoid getting into fights, and how to get along with parents. The other script that I gave you, the Tackling School Problems Scene, is probably most applicable to our work here at Central."

Seeing the Teacher.

Introduction. Almost everyone has run into some difficulties with at least a few courses in school. Either the teacher doesn't seem to explain things clearly enough, or the course seems unimportant to our later lives, or some other problem comes up. While everyone has experienced these difficulties at one time or other, some people seem to be able to solve school problems better than others. Others let these problems ride until they are really behind in the course and have a bad attitude toward the course and school in general. It is hard for a person to remain interested in school and want to continue going to school when he is getting farther and farther behind and not trying to solve the various school problems as they arise.

One of the best ways of solving school problems is to tackle them as soon as they appear. This should be done by talking over course problems with the teacher. To insure that a talk with the teacher is helpful, the following rules are worthwhile to keep in mind:

1. Don't put off these discussions. Go as soon as the problem arises.

2. Have a specific problem in mind. A teacher can only help you when you are able to talk clearly about the things that are giving you trouble.

3. Don't just dump the whole problem in the teacher's lap and expect it to be solved. Follow through on his suggestions.

Scene A. In the scenes today, you'll see the right way and the wrong way to talk out a school problem with a teacher. In both scenes, the boy is having trouble with math and has come in to see his teacher. In the first scene, Mr. ____ and I will act out the wrong way. It is too bad, but probably a lot of discussions with teachers turn out to be as unsuccessful as this one.

Teacher: Come in, Bob. Did you want to see me?

Bob: Yeah, I'm having an awful lot of trouble with your course and I thought I'd better come in and see you since we're going to have an exam in a couple of days.

Teacher: Well, I'll be glad to try and help. What's giving you trouble?

Bob: (laughing and shrugging his shoulders) Well . . . math.

Teacher: (smiling) Maybe you can pin it down better than that.

Bob: I don't know. I guess I haven't understood much from the second chapter on.

Teacher: Well, now, Bob, we finished that chapter over four weeks ago. If you didn't understand something in chapter two, you should have come in then when you started to have difficulties.

Bob: Yeah, I guess so, but I thought maybe I'd catch on after awhile. But now I don't know. It seems to be getting worse all the time.

Teacher: I don't know if I can be of much help now. The material in chapter nine and in chapter ten that I assigned today is pretty much impossible to understand if you didn't get the concepts in the previous chapters. Are you reading the book as we go along in class? Are you up to where the rest of the class is?

Bob: No, not really. I just sort of gave up after chapter four.

Teacher: Are you having trouble understanding the book? Does it make sense to you when you read it?

Bob: No, it's pretty heavy -- hard to understand. And I haven't
          understood much of what you've said in class lately either.

Teacher: I think what we'd better do is to get you up with the basic
          concepts and then try to catch you up with the class. Now,
          we don't use this book, but it has the same material. Some
          people find it easier to understand. What you should do is
          to read the first four chapters in it and try to understand
          that material and then come in and see me again and we'll
          talk over any problems you've had with it. Then maybe you
          can start again in the regular text and read chapters five
          through ten. I think they'll make better sense to you then.
          And remember to work a couple of problems at the end of each
          section that you read. If anything gives you trouble, bring
          it along with you when you come in to see me.

Bob: Boy, that's an awful lot of work. I don't know if I'm gonna
          have time to do that by Friday.

Teacher: Yes, it's going to take extra effort on your part to catch up.
          But it's not too bad. You don't have to work all the problems
          and the new book will go fairly fast, I think. I'll let you
          skip the exam Friday. You can take a make-up when you get
          caught up.

Bob: Well, I didn't expect when I came in here that I'd have more
          work to do. I kind of had some plans lined up for the next
          few weekends.

Teacher: Now, Bob, if you're going to catch up and make a passing grade
          in my class, you'll have to sacrifice something. After all,
          you've let this problem slip too long. You should have come
          in right away when you first started having trouble.

Bob: Yeah, I know. Well, I guess I know what I hafta do if I want
          to pass the test.

Discussion points. 1. How helpful was the teacher? Is it likely that
Bob's problem is solved by having gone to him? Is this a difficult solution and is there an easier way? 2. Do you think that Bob feels any more
favorably disposed toward math after having talked to the teacher? Do
you think the teacher thinks Bob is very interested in math? 3. Emphasize
the fact that avoidance behavior is not an effective coping technique
even though it produces some short-term relief.

Scene B. The setting of this scene is the same as Scene A.

Teacher: Come in, Bob. Did you want to see me?

Bob: Yeah, I'm having trouble with this section that you assigned yesterday, and I thought I'd better come in and see you before I got messed up.

Teacher: I'm glad you did. Have you read the section?

Bob: Yeah, I read it last night, but I didn't understand it too well. When I went to work these problems here at the end, I couldn't get anywhere with them. Could you work through this example problem here? This is where I really got fouled up.

Teacher: Yes, of course. How have you been doing up to now?

Bob: Okay. I thought everything was okay until I got to this stuff.

Teacher: I'm glad you came in early before you started to really get behind. This is an important section and the material in it is necessary for the things we'll be studying for the rest of the course. But this section must be a lot harder to understand than the rest. I've had about four people come in and ask me for help with this assignment.

Bob: Really? I thought I was the only one having problems.

Teacher: Oh, no. As a matter of fact, it's a good thing that you are all coming in and asking about it. I had planned to give a quiz on this section tomorrow to see if you are all keeping up with the work. But if some of you are having trouble understanding this section, there's no use testing you on it.

Bob: Geez, I couldn't pass a test on this stuff.

Teacher: Well, I plan instead to spend tomorrow going over the section step-by-step, since it's giving so many people trouble.

Bob: Yeah, that'd probably be better.

Teacher: Also, if you want, you could read these three pages in this other book by Walters. He has a better explanation of what's going on than our textbook.

Bob: Yeah, okay. I can do that in study hall and get the book back to you right away.

Teacher: That's fine. Now about this sample problem, let me explain it as I work it on the board.

Discussion points. 1. Is this brown-nosing? What would make it like "buttering up" the teacher? 2. What other problems might be tackled by talking them over with a teacher? 3. Does Bob feel like a "dummy" because he asks the teacher for help? How would you feel? Would your expectations of how your friends might see this prevent you from trying to get help from a teacher? (Sarason & Ganzer, 1971, pp. 136-138).

"There is one other thing I should mention," Bill added. "At the end of the series of 15 meetings, the boys were asked to write scripts of their own and to serve as the models in enacting them. Not only was this a creative experience for them, but they came up with some excellent scripts."

Mary Clay had another question, "Who came up with the ideas for the topics of these scripts, and how were the scripts developed?" Bill replied, "I can explain that. First, the researchers spent several weeks conducting informal rap sessions with small groups of boys at the institution, focusing on the boys' problems and how they viewed them, their feelings about adults, their peers, the worlds of education and work, and things like that. The sessions were tape recorded so the researchers could study them and pick out relevant material for modeling topics.

"The next step was to get the boys' ideas of different ways of coping with the problems that had been identified through the group discussions. The various problem-solving behaviors were illustrated in groups through role-playing procedures. The role-playing sessions were also tape recorded. A number of them provided such good illustrations of problem-solving behavior that they were transcribed into preliminary scripts which later were used in the modeling groups. Also, some scripts were written by the researchers, but all of them were critiqued and modified wherever necessary by both the models and the participating boys."

Mary Clay now seemed to be ready for action. "Let's write some scripts of our own -- and let's get the kids to do the same. I think we're ready for one or two trial runs right here at Central. I know there's a lot of scientific information we don't have right this minute, but, with good sense, I think we can put the ideas we have to good use."

Mary's challenge was taken up during the remainder of the meeting, at several subsequent ones, and at one evening working session at Bill Bennett' house. The group realized that it would be unwise to move too fast. They soon saw that the problem was how to mesh general principles of behavior (for instance, those related to modeling) with the facts of life at Central.

The Central Squares

Bill, with the help of his colleagues, instituted the first GAM action program. Part of his job as a school counselor was to keep in touch with many students who were frequent absentees or potential or actual dropouts. One way he had hit upon for doing this was to organize a group (whose number fluctuated widely depending on such variables as how the kids felt and the state of the weather) that would be interesting enough to its members to make them want to maintain some tie -- albeit a tenuous one -- with Central High School. There were about 20 youngsters in the group. They had in common their alienation from the traditional academic pursuits. Beyond that, they were a diverse group -- boys, girls, very bright kids, kids who had trouble handling school work, kids who wanted jobs but couldn't get them, and quiet boys and girls who just didn't seem to be interested in school.

The group met three afternoons a week from one to three. There was nothing that could be called a curriculum. Everything was informal, with a considerable portion of the time devoted to talking and sharing experiences. Bill provided information about school and job requirements. Often Bill served as a sounding board for their ideas. Everybody at Central recognized that the cement that held together the Central Squares (the name the group somehow gave itself) was Bill's personality and the trust that students and ex-students felt in him.

Bill's idea was to add a little structure to the Central Squares meetings. He invited three likeable, high-prestige, high-achieving students to the group for 45 minutes twice a week. (Because these students were so capable, and because he was able to make a case for their participation in Central Squares as being developmentally valuable for them, he was able to arrange their "released time" from normal school programs.) The peer models also were active in extracurricular activities (football team, swimming team, student government) and were selected by Bill because of their leadership abilities and desire to help others.

Bill tried a number of different approaches -- often at the same time. There were some free-wheeling discussions, but more and more Bill veered toward reasonably well-organized modeling and role-playing sessions. Getting scripts and ideas for scripts was no easy matter. Most of the ones they began with were revisions made by Bill of scripts he had uncovered in his reading. Each session began with enactments by peer leaders, followed by discussion among teams of peer leaders and group members, and concluded with role-playing by the group members themselves. The atmosphere of the meetings was always businesslike. Bill helped the peer leaders to understand that a no-nonsense, task-oriented approach would be much more helpful than an approach that encouraged the group members to feel sorry for themselves.

At first, the Central Squares were passively resistant to the peer leaders and to Bill. The peer leaders, having been forewarned by Bill, were not surprised when this happened. Working in their favor was the fact that the Central Squares had little self-respect, and not far below their abrasive surfaces they admired the strong, confident kids who had joined their group. After several meetings everybody seemed to enjoy the modeling-role-playing session. Attendance stabilized at a higher level and one dropout actually returned to school on an almost regular basis.

After a while Bill had an insight. "Why can't the Squares identify the problems that are of special concern to them and do their own script

writing?" He asked the question one afternoon and found himself intrigued by the discussion that ensued. First there was a flood of suggestions about how the "borrowed" scripts they were using could be improved.
With the leadership of Bill and one of the peer models (a swimmer),
the group decided to see what they could do. They made a list and put
at the top the temptation to cut class or drop out of school. Bill divided the group into teams and gave each some scripts from the delin-
quency project for ideas. He agreed to serve as consultant to the
groups but kept as much in the background as he could.

For a week-and-a-half the Squares focused intensively on the dropout,
why he stops coming to school and how he might be reclaimed. As the
groups produced their scripts, they were read, discussed, and enacted
by the whole group. As they discussed their productions, almost everyone
became involved in the nuances of their acting and what the persons whose
roles they were playing had actually said. Bill felt that even the most
bored and socially inadequate member of the Squares was actually attending to the scripts as dramatic material and to the problem of avoiding
the temptation to drop out. Another thing Bill noticed was that the
Squares were becoming a more cohesive group. As each day passed it
seemed that the boys and girls were surrendering one of their defenses:
criticism of the material they were working with. Instead the meetings
were increasingly more constructive. They began to ask such questions
as: What can you really say to the guy who is quitting school? How do
you answer your friends when they invite you to cut class?

Team A and Team B worked together on the first script which was one of
special interest to all Squares.

Dropping Out

Introduction. Dropping out is perhaps one of the biggest problems most
schools are facing today. Many students having difficulties or problems
in school find it much easier to avoid them by dropping out. Often, many
of their friends are influenced and follow suit. Life out of school
seems fun and carefree. Thinking of the future is easily avoidable.
This situation focuses on the pressure for many students to drop out.

Scene. Don is shooting pool with one of his dropout friends, Fred, at
a local pool hall near the school.

Don: Wow, nice shot, Fred, you win again.

Fred: Nothing to it, practice makes perfect.

Don: Hey, I'd better get going, class will start in a few minutes.

Fred: What's the rush? Don't you want to try to even up?

Don: I don't have the time; maybe later, after school.

Fred: Looks like they've really got you hung up. You know school's
         a big waste of time. You don't learn anything. Besides, you're
         not doing too hot in there anyway.

Don: Maybe not, but I'm still going.

Fred: Look, Bill's meeting me in a few minutes. We're going to shoot
         some pins. C'mon and join us and forget about school.

Don: I've already told you, I can't make it.

Fred: What are you up tight about? You don't need school and they
         don't need you. It's just a big trip. Why wait to flunk out?

Don: Listen, man, it's tough enough trying to find a job with a high
         school diploma. I'm not stupid enough to try it without one.
         Maybe I'm not doing too good, but I'll still get through.

Fred: Who needs it. I didn't get through and I don't have a job, but
         I'm doing okay.

Don: Sure, you're living off your folks, but my mom's sick again and
         my ol' man's still not working. He's been trying for months to
         find a job. It's a rough world; I need all the breaks I can get
         and getting through school is going to be a big one. Once I
         have that diploma, life is going to be much easier.

Fred: Yeah, I guess so.

Don: I'll see you later, all right?

Fred: All right.

Discussion points. 1. Discuss Fred's feelings toward school. 2. How
does Don feel about school? 3. What caused Don to resist the temptations
that Fred offered? 4. Is school important? 5. Discuss other possible
pressures to drop out of school.

Even though everyone recognized that the script could be improved in different ways, complaints about unrealistic scripts became fewer. The
Squares were becoming more task oriented and, perhaps most importantly,
they were identifying more and more with the goal of the group: to
increase the student's effectiveness in and enjoyment of school. An
example of the progress made was a script written by Team A to cope with
a happily increasing "problem": how to say "No" to a classmate who wants
to borrow your homework. For the Squares, of course, this was a relatively novel experience.

Team A: Doing Homework

Scene: Two students, Fred and Joe, are sitting together in the school
cafeteria eating lunch. They both have the same class right after the
noon period.

Fred: You do the assignment?

Joe: Yep.

Fred: How's about letting me copy it?

Joe: What? You didn't do it again?

Fred: No.

Joe: I'm always letting you copy my answers; why don't you try doing
        it yourself once in a while?

Fred: I've been pretty busy. I really don't have much time to work
        them out. Besides you always get it done; you've got time to
        do them.

Joe: Cut it out. I'm just as busy as you are. I find time to do
        the work and you can do the same thing.

Fred: How?

Joe: Listen, every night, I put aside a set time to do my work. I
        don't plan anything else for that time. That way I don't have
        anything to distract me. I don't let it go like I used to. This
        way I don't avoid it.

Fred: Yeah, but that's tough to do.

Joe: Its just like dinner time. You eat dinner at a set time every
        night. You're used to that. It's the same thing. You can get
        used to doing schoolwork at a certain time every night too.

Fred: Sounds like it might work.

Joe: It does. I work for two hours and that's it. No one bothers
        me at home because they know at that time I'll be studying.

Fred: Hmmmmmmmm.........Could I still borrow your paper?

Joe: Nope, you can't borrow it every time; you'd better start making
        time yourself.

Fred: Yeah, ... maybe I'll have to.

Discussion points. 1. Should Joe have loaned his paper to Fred? Why or why not? 2. Is it possible for you to set up a time like Joe did to study? Discuss the reasons. 3. What can you do to insure that once having set a specific time, you'd follow it?

One of the problems that often arose during the Squares' discussions was the difficulty some students had in concentrating and organizing their day so as to complete homework assignments without "ruining" their lives. This was Team B's approach to that problem:

Team B: Doing Homework

Introduction. One problem that many of us have is in getting our school work done. Often we avoid doing it until the last minute. Then we either do a poor job or we don't do it at all. Once having gotten behind in a class, we may find it hard to catch up. There's a tendency then to just let go any work in that class. Perhaps the key idea is to get it done early. This scene shows examples of how to deal more effectively with this problem.

Scene: John and Charley are high school students who have just come out of class. They are at their lockers when the following discussion takes place.

John: You get that paper in?

Charley: Yeah, you?

John: Nah.

Charley: Hey, that was a really important paper. She really wanted us to get that done.

John: I know . . . I guess I'm behind in that class.

Charley: You should watch it; that ol' Mrs. Sharpe is pretty rough. She really pushes the class. What's the matter, you've got a problem?

John: Well, you know, I've been sort of busy lately. I'm usually down at Jake's Place messing around. Say, aren't you behind, too? I see you down there all the time.

Charley: I'm there almost every day but I'm doing all right in class. I'm not behind or anything.

John: What's your secret, man?

Charley: No secret, I just get it done.

John: Like when?

Charley: As soon as I get home from school, I study for a couple of hours and that leaves my evenings free.

John: Wow, look at the straight student. C'mon, you didn't use to be like that.

Charley: Yeah, I used to mess around all the time too and then after I'd gotten home I'd still watch TV. After that I'd be tired and too sleepy to do any schoolwork. Then I'd feel guilty as heck for not doing it. I'd tell myself, I'll make up for it tomorrow but I never did.

John: Yeah, that sounds like me.

Charley: So, I decided to study after school every day for a couple of hours. It was kind of hard to do at first because I wasn't used to it but I began to think of it as part of school. You know, like a study hall or something. The only difference was that for me, school's not out until five. Thinking about it that way made it easier.

John: It works, huh?

Charley: It really surprised me. I'm doing better in school. But the best thing about it is right after five, I can mess around all I want without thinking about it. You should try it.

John: Maybe I will.

Discussion points. 1. Compare your feelings after completing schoolwork to that of not having completed it. 2. Charley suggested that "guilt" feelings are involved. Is that true of you? 3. What's the value of doing schoolwork? What activities keep you from doing your work and can they be delayed?

In addition to the Squares' heightened interest in writing and enacting scripts, Bill noticed some healthy developments concerning the peer models. Before and after the modeling sessions, the peer leaders and group members had more and more informal conversations. They seemed to be getting to know and like each other. In the third week, one peer leader and a group member got together to outline the topic and script for a later session. It is significant that all of the work of this team took place outside of school time. In training the peer leaders, Bill had placed special stress on their reinforcing (with praise, interest, a smile) responses by group members that seemed to be positive, adaptive, and a step in the right direction. This pair of script writers became mutually reinforcing. Lonnie Jackson, the leader, glowed every time he got Mark Fletcher to say something indicating that it really wasn't a bad idea to plan for the future. Reciprocally, Mark soon came to feel that Lonnie, a football star, really was interested in him and that he personally liked him. Mark, who had wanted to play on the Central team, had tried out but hadn't been big enough or good enough to make it. He had been certain that football players did nothing but play football, strut around like big shots, and let the admiration of others slide off their backs. Mark, at first, was surprised to learn that Lonnie was not on leave from Mt. Olympus but was an O.K. guy with ideas, a sense of humor, and a willingness to work hard.

Another side benefit was the decision by the group after five weeks to form an activities club. Twice a month they would do something together -- things like visiting a factory, union headquarters, a museum, or a police precinct. The peer leaders went along on these trips and were especially good models because they asked the right questions of the people they visited and encouraged the group members to ask questions and make comments. Bill helped by arranging the visits and the transportation.

Another thing happened. After the first Central Squares member decided to return to school, the peer leaders made it clear that they would set up a special catch-up tutoring program for each returnee. In some cases, the peer leaders used their friends as "consultants" in working with the returnees. The peer leaders had decided that it might help if they and the returnees spent some time doing homework together even when there was nothing to talk over and tutoring was not needed.

All felt that Bill's program was a success. There were rough spots, mistakes (by Bill, as well as the peer leaders), and anxious moments (as when one group member said he had heard that Lonnie Jackson smoked marijuana). Nevertheless, Bill was proud of both his group and his peer leaders. As word spread of the success of the Central Squares, everybody connected with it got his share of accolades. One of the most satisfying moments for Bill came when the principal, Jim Penney, met with the group to let them know he appreciated all they were doing. Bill was especially pleased to discover that Lonnie Jackson had told Jim that as a result of working with the Squares program he was thinking about becoming a school counselor or social worker.

V. TEACHERS CAN MODEL, TOO

As the school year pushed on, the GAM began to reap dividends from the time and work devoted to the notions of modeling and role-playing. Numerous anecdotal reports of teachers using modeling in their own classrooms were cause for justifiable satisfaction. The GAM meetings continued on a regular basis and dealt with a variety of topics: how teachers could function more effectively as models for students, relevant articles and books uncovered by group members, and why modeling worked (when it did work, that is, since everyone recognized that it wasn't a cure-all).

Out of an early GAM discussion of an article Harriet Schultz had brought to the attention of the group, an interest crystallized in teachers' learning to be better teachers through the observation of effective models. The group took two tacks. One involved identifying especially able teachers. The identification could not be accomplished in a highly objective way, but every GAM member could suggest the names of one or two very able colleagues at Central or one of the other city schools. Informal meetings were arranged, and the guests (the model teachers) talked about how they approached particular problems. These meetings were valuable even though often what the Central teachers acquired was not a recipe for solving particular problems. For example, Jack Fahey, a white teacher at a predominantly black school, told the GAM about one of the most important ingredients for survival in a situation such as the one in his school. This ingredient was for the white teacher to accept the reality of racial differences and to avoid being too preoccupied or serious about them. The GAM members felt less uptight about their jobs after talking with Jack Fahey.

The other tack involved finding and discussing written descriptions of how particular teachers had succeeded in school situations where the odds didn't appear favorable. Harriet Schultz uncovered one of the best accounts in a pamphlet by Jablonsky (1972) entitled, There are some good teachers of the disadvantaged. Jablonsky, using an informal method of identifying especially adept teachers similar to that used by the GAM in the city schools, visited the teachers' classrooms and spoke with them at length. Jablonsky found that charisma is not the hallmark of the teacher who is successful with disadvantaged children. Many of these teachers are quiet and reserved. They have an inner strength that is readily recognized by observers, and it is that strength and the skills and knowledge they bring to their tasks that children respond to. Many of the teachers visited by Jablonsky reported childhood experiences which involved exposure to poverty, injustice, fear, and frustration. Having outwardly overcome these handicaps, or at least having learned how to live with them, seemed to equip these teachers with the radar needed to hear and interpret the signals they get from the tensions and unhappiness of their students.

The GAM felt that, valuable as it was to read about or actually meet especially able teachers, it was necessary to do some modeling and role-playing themselves. One of the unanticipated gains of the regular discussions of modeling was this realization that teachers, counselors, school psychologists, and administrators might themselves get something out of observing and responding to models. Mary Clay pointed out, "After all, what is modeling other than providing certain types of information for people? Modeled information simply shows an observer how someone else handles a particular situation." Her comments were provocative because they served to place modeling in a realistic context -- one dimension of the process of information transmission.

Some teachers were better than others in solving specific classroom problems. This was easy enough to accept in the abstract. Everybody knows that there are individual differences in teacher effectiveness. Could teachers and other school personnel who are less able in some respects learn from observing teachers who are more able? And perhaps just as important, would they be willing to learn?

Bill Bennett thought he knew the answer, or, as it turned out, answers. First, how could they ever arrange things so that they could observe each other teach and handle specific problems? Each school employee -- be he a teacher, administrator or pupil personnel worker -- had a full-time program. Time couldn't be taken from the teachers' full classroom program to permit them to visit an Oscar performance in a classroom down the hall. There were all sorts of practical problems connected with teachers observing teachers. It almost made modeling for students seem an easy matter.

"But you know," Bill thought out loud, "maybe the biggest problem is that most of us would feel pretty uneasy about spying on our colleagues and having them spy on us. It wouldn't be spying, of course -- after all, we would be doing it voluntarily. But some of us will be better than others. I'm not that much of a masochist that I want everybody to see what a lousy job I do."

The group spent several session doing what the counselors and psychologists call working through a problem. They refused to run away from the notion of doing some modeling for themselves. Going for them was the fact that they had come to feel quite comfortable as a group and trusted each other. On their side also was a strong desire to develop exemplary programs at Central. They were encouraged by how the students had reacted to modeling, and decided to take the plunge.

The way they did it was to meet once a week to conduct what Bill Bennett called simulation sessions. Each session dealt with a classroom problem that seemed important to at least a few teachers. (The GAM membership had by now more than tripled to a total of 20). A team of two or three teachers would plan a week ahead, role-play the problem situation, and model what they regarded as a reasonable approach to it. The teachers who did the modeling were usually teachers who felt fairly sure of themselves in problem situations. Some of the modeling had to do with seemingly straightforward skills such as maintaining eye contact when talking with someone. Others involved quite general aspects of human relationships, such as showing the other person that you are attentive to what he is saying. Still others were peculiar to life in school. For example, several teachers modeled different ways of dealing with students who are belligerent and disruptive in class. One young male teacher modeled the role of an aggressive student, and several other teachers took turns modeling the ways that they would deal with this problem in the classroom. One important principle that emerged from this modeling exercise was that power confrontations between teacher and student should be avoided, especially in the presence of the student's peers.

Some meetings were kicked off by a faculty member presenting a fictitious problem. The task for each group member would be to analyze it from the standpoint of modeling and, perhaps, model a solution if one came to mind.

After each simulation session, a discussion was held about the likely effectiveness of the modeled approach to the problem. Sometimes there were ideas and controversies about better or different approaches to the problem. When this happened, they were modeled on the spot. In any event, most persons present at the meeting took their turns as models. Not everyone felt confident about his performance. Far from it. It came as a surprise to some teachers that, even though their enactments might be terrible, they nevertheless felt good afterwards. Fran Hardy, after feeling she had looked silly modeling how to be firm with a student who was always testing the limits, made this comment, "Somehow, making all those silly mistakes in front of you makes me feel good. I think it's because you are getting to see me as I really am and you aren't rejecting me for it."

Modeling like this gives the budding teacher an opportunity to observe directly what teaching is all about. Practice or cadet teaching is based in part on this idea. Besides the method used at Central High, other techniques are possible, limited only by the ingenuity of each school's staff. Videotape recordings of the behavior of experienced teachers in both simulated and actual classroom situations provide the teacher-in-training with a wider range of experiences than would be possible in practice teaching assignments of relatively short duration. The use of television, of course, need not be limited to viewing. When videotaping facilities are available several expanded opportunities present themselves:

1) The teacher-in-training can replay as often as is necessary all or selected parts of a master teacher's tape library.

2) He can observe tape-recordings of himself in various kinds of simulated or actual classroom settings.

3) He can observe himself progressively on videotape as he gradually gains mastery of particular situations that are difficult for him.

The key concepts that serve to integrate all of the material presented in this and earlier sections are information and informational feedback. Modeling provides information about the world and situations concerning which individuals may lack experience or feel inadequate. Informational feedback provides information to the individual about his own behavior. Feedback can be obtained either directly through observing videotapes of ones' own behavior or through reactions of others to our reactions, as, for example, in behavioral rehearsal. Observation of others and ourselves can be a significant experience educationally, vocationally, and socially.

Some Hints About Observational Learning in the Classroom

Several important points growing out of research on modeling principles bear particularly on classroom practice:

1. Define the type of behavior to be modeled as explicitly as you can (for instance, persisting after an initial attempt at solving a problem fails, being patient, expressing anger and annoyance tactfully).

2. Before instituting a modeling program, plan where, when and how often you should make the type of response you hope your students will emulate.

3. Check the frequency of students' responses to be modeled before instituting the modeling program.

4. Check the frequency of students' responses to be modeled after instituting the modeling program.

5. Check your ideas, plans, and procedures with colleagues who will not be too polite to give you frank criticisms and useful suggestions. (Often there is no absolutely "best" behavior in a given situation).

6. Think about the problem of getting the students to attend to (listen and watch) the modeled response.

7. Consider such tactical alternatives as the use of teacher or peer models, and whether or not the modeling should be done with a well-structured format. Models should be selected on the basis of what response is to be modeled. But, in some circumstances, the most effective model may not be available. In that case improvisation is required.

8. Decide on the place of practice trials (behavior rehearsal) in role-playing in your modeling. In some cases, observations of modeled behavior without behavior rehearsal will be sufficient. However, rehearsal is usually a worthwhile component.

9. Consider the question of the role of reinforcement in the program. Should either the model or the observers or both receive reinforcements for emitting desired responses? Reinforcements (e.g., praise) increase a student's interest level and motivation to learn new response patterns. We tend to remember behavior that "pays off."

10. As the program progresses, rethink it periodically. Should new modeled responses be added to the observational learning repertory? Can it be improved or strengthened? When nonproductive patterns of activity or job performance persist, look for the presence of undesirable models or rewards.

Becoming More Expert in the Use of Modeling and Role-Playing

For many readers this pamphlet is only a beginning. Your school or school district might wish to consider the possibility of conducting a workshop on modeling. In some instances certain school personnel, such as a school psychologist or counselor, may have special expertise which can be communicated to others. Outside consultants often are especially helpful in conducting workshops. Your local school district or state department of education probably can help you find outside consultants and to plan a workshop or an in-service program.

Modeling can be a powerful technique in teaching -- the cadet teacher learns from observing the master teacher, and students learn from observing their teachers and peers. Learning to be skillful in changing undesirable behavior through behavior modification often comes about through observational learning. Practice in the use of modeling, either in the classroom or as an adjunct to classroom activities, adds polish and confidence to the teacher's or counselor's behavior.

Would you like to try your hand at modeling? If so, here are two sample problems. Devise your own modeling and role-playing procedures. Remember there are no cut-and-dried answers.

1. Martha Jones has never had more than one or two black children in her class. Now, because of redrawn district lines, 14 of her 37 eleven- and twelve-year-olds are black. Mrs. Jones is somewhat uncertain about the social relationships among the children under these circumstances. She is concerned that there may be black-white factionalism and antagonism.

(Might Mrs. Jones consider asking the children to model both white and black roles as a means of breaking down racial barriers?)

2. Jerry Neal's classroom is the noisiest one in the school. The children talk loudly and often out of turn. Although aware of this unproductive state of affairs, Mr. Neal doesn't know what to do about it. A colleague commented one day that Mr. Neal certainly must have a pair of healthy lungs judging from the booming voice with which

he summoned his kids after recess. Afterwards, Mr. Neal wondered whether a connection might exist between the level of his oral expressiveness and that of his students.

(Could it be that the model which Mr. Neal provides his students might be improved? If so, how?)

VI. MODELING FOR VOCATIONAL TRAINING

The focus of this pamphlet has been on observational learning as a general
aid to teachers, counselors, administrators and other school personnel.
It is this very generality that permits its adaptation and application to
meet specific needs in educational and other spheres. The following example did not come from a school setting, but it illustrates how modeling
can be applied to the important topics of vocational education and vocational training. In the example, a girl is being helped by a therapist
to deal more effectively with the crucial job interview, failure in which
can limit personal growth regardless of the individual's actual ability:

> Jane, a recent high school graduate, had just been refused employment
> on two job interviews. Being rather timid and nonassertive, Jane was
> disappointed and on the verge of crying when she came to the group
> meeting. She stated that there was another job-opening in her neigh-
> borhood but she was fearful of being rejected a third time. Jane's
> closest friend, Mabel, was also in the group. Mabel was already
> working. At the suggestion of the therapist she was willing to play
> the part of job applicant and the therapist played the employer's
> part. Jane was told to watch closely as Mabel played her (Jane's)
> part. Mabel played the part well and the therapist asked Jane then
> to review exactly what Mabel did. With some hesitation Jane then
> began her rehearsal by saying, "I saw the 'girl wanted' sign in the
> window." But when she was asked if she could work until seven, Jane
> appeared tense and offered no response. When Louise prompted her with
> some suggestions, Jane was better able to answer and after practice
> with more unexpected questions, Jane gradually became more comfort-
> able. The therapist responded initially with smiles and compliments
> to her assertive responses but gradually became more businesslike
> and less pleasant. At the last trial the group applauded her efforts
> and Jane beamed. Jane's behavioral assignment was to apply for the
> job the next day. The therapist announced to Jane that he expected
> her to report on the outcome of the interview at the next meeting.
> She was relieved to know that if the interview did not work she
> could continue practicing for other interviews (Rose, 1972, p. 124).

Vocational education is an important facet of all educational programs.
But it is, perhaps, of greatest value to persons who are members of several
large special groups.

One of these consists of youngsters who come from severely disadvantaged
backgrounds. The middle-class child, because of his economic advantages
and the profusion of successful models available to him, usually develops
enough self-confidence and skill in presenting himself (and his qualifi-
cations) to others that he adequately handles such encounters as job
interviews. A youngster with less going for him is, understandably, often
more hesitant and less able to put his best foot forward. Sometimes this

occurs because the disadvantaged person does not really understand what the interviewer is looking for as he conducts the interview. Vocationally oriented programs typically focus on information concerning types of jobs, the opportunities available, job prerequisites and preparation, and the possibilities for advancement. These are major topics that must be included in any program aimed at helping the young person develop realistic goals and training. Another element is the concept of work and his perception of himself as a worker.

This facet of vocational development is especially important in the case of the person who bears some of the stigma not only of inadequate socio-economic opportunities but also of past misdeeds. How might the juvenile delinquent, perhaps incarcerated for his misdeeds, be helped to attain an adequate vocational adjustment? It is all well and good for him to be given vocational information, but if he is unsure and worried about how to account to a job interviewer for the time spent in an institution or for his criminal record, it is going to be difficult for him to put the information to good use. Modeling and behavior rehearsal can help strengthen his ability to handle potentially traumatic situations such as job interviews.

Frank, a 17-year-old boy, attended a large multiracial high school in a lower socioeconomic neighborhood. Despite a desperate financial situation, his mother deeply hoped that he would obtain a high school diploma (his father had left home when Frank was quite small). Unfortunately, as worry turned to desperation, Frank decided that he had to get a job in the hope of bettering life for his mother and younger brother and sisters. How could he drop out of school? Frank thought about that question and wondered who would care if he simply stopped coming to school. Some of his friends and a few teachers might take note of his absence, but the void created by his absence would soon be filled. Frank finally mentioned his predicament to an English teacher he liked and to whom he felt he could talk. Frank had never gotten more than a C on any of this teacher's exams or assignments, but had sensed a sincere interest on the part of this teacher and a willingness to listen.

The teacher expressed regret at Frank's decision but didn't try to talk him out of it. Instead he told Frank that if he did leave school the possibility still existed that he could get a diploma through special programs in operation in the school district. What the teacher did empha-size was the importance of getting as good and as interesting a job as possible. When Frank expressed some anxieties about being interviewed by personnel people who wouldn't think much of his skills, the teacher strongly urged him to talk to John Harris, one of the school's counselors.

John Harris had seen many kids like Frank, kids who didn't have the vaguest idea of how to present themselves and their assets effectively to a disinterested outsider. When Mr. Harris saw how scared Frank was, he realized that a few words of advice would not do the trick. He decided that the most direct course of action would be to demonstrate some sali-ent aspects of self-presentation for Frank. Picking a number of situations

Frank was likely to have to confront, Mr. Harris modeled a variety of response patterns. These included putting himself in the best possible light but not overselling his assets, stressing to the personnel person the importance he attached to getting a job with a future, and saying more than once that he was willing to work hard in acquiring skills. Mr. Harris met with Frank on two occasions. During the first one, Mr. Harris was a one man band playing both roles -- personnel person and Frank. During the second session, he played the job interviewer and Frank played himself. Mr. Harris was completely business-like, pointing out Frank's effective and ineffective behavior. When Frank's ineffectiveness changed to effectiveness, he gave Frank an opportunity for behavior rehearsal, practice at playing his effective roles.

At the end of the second session, before he wished him well, Mr. Harris reviewed for Frank the opportunities open to him for ultimately getting a diploma. What Mr. Harris did by way of modeling job interviewing skills for Frank was not a controlled experiment. Still, the fact is that Frank was able to get a full-time job in a supermarket not far from his home. Frank was sure that the confidence he acquired from observing Mr. Harris' modeling and from his own role-playing helped him to be more impressive and comfortable in the job interview situation. Frank never did return to school, and he did not get a diploma. However, he not only held his job, but over the years he was moved up to assistant manager of another store in the supermarket chain.

VII. A REVIEW OF MODELING PRINCIPLES AND PRACTICES

As they learned and practiced modeling, the GAM tried to collate information they had gathered and to organize their knowledge. Much of their knowledge focused on such questions as: When to use modeling? How to use modeling?

Since modeling is not a cure-all, it is necessary to inquire into the conditions under which it is likely to be educationally and developmentally helpful. Modeling can be helpful when (1) there is a clear picture of what a student is doing that is maladaptive; (2) there is reasonable certainty that substitute behaviors would improve the student's adjustment.

An important step in modeling is demonstration. Modeling will be ineffective if the student is not attending to the model. In setting up a demonstration, the behaviors to be learned should be clearly and simply specified and salient features of the modeling scene pointed out. Among the salient features are any rewards (positive reinforcements) given to the model for his exemplary behavior, and the rewards that might be given to the observer who emulates the model's behavior. It is helpful to encourage students to think about, rehearse, and practice in his everyday life the behavior demonstrated in a modeling session.

The elements of modeling generally can be organized as follows:

1. Attention. To insure attention on the part of students, the teacher or counselor must attend to these questions:

   a) What are the model's characteristics?

   b) What incentives are at work in the modeling situation?

   c) What is the modeling stimulus; that is, what is the behavior being demonstrated?

   d) Is this behavior clearly observable?

   e) What are the characteristics of the observers?

2. Role-playing or behavior rehearsal.

   a) What level of complexity or perfection in role-playing is feasible or desirable?

   b) Do the role-players require any special skills? (Obviously, the fewer special skills required, the better.)

3. Retention and transfer of training.

   a) Has the modeling and role-playing been arranged so as to increase the likelihood that the observers and role-players will think about and covertly rehearse what they learned in the modeling session?

   b) Can the observers practice what they have learned in their lives? If so, how?

4. Motivation.

   a) What incentives are at work in the life of the student that will increase the likelihood of his using the new behavior?

   b) Can special incentives (reinforcements) be added to school life to motivate students to adopt modeled behavior that they have role-played.

VIII. A FINAL WORD

Everyone wants to know "How do you do it?" "What should I say when she says 'No'?" "How can I show him I'm interested?" We have seen that observing and hearing models who display behavior we desire to add to our repertory can be very helpful. Copying or imitating desired behavior is neither the only nor necessarily the best way of increasing adeptness in interpersonal relationships. For some purposes, a sink-or-swim, trial-and-error approach may well be the method of choice. The youngster who is a non-swimmer and does manage to get to shore after having been thrown into the middle of the lake might well feel gratified at his achievement. However, this does not mean that he should not take lessons and observe carefully the swimming behavior of an aquatic instructor.

While it is important that people learn to figure things out for themselves, it is equally important that their questions be answered and they be shown examples of desired behavior. The following example, taken from Ele and Walt Dulaney's newspaper column mentioned earlier, is humorous to us, but nonetheless refers to a problem that is a serious one for Joe and many other young people:

Dear Walt: I don't smoke and I'm wondering if I have a right to ask my dates not to smoke in my car. I don't like the smell and it stays in the car for a long, long time after the smokers go.
-Joe

Dear Joe: You have the right, but exercise it at point of invitation. "I'm really bothered by cigaret smoke, so I've made my car nicotine-free by banning cigarets. I'd love to take you to the concert (dance, whatever), but I don't know if you can stand the drive without a puff. What do you think?"

If she says "yes," remind her of her promise by posting a cancer-control sign on the dashboard. (Hurrah for you!)
-Walt
(Seattle Times, November 6, 1972)

Joe wrote to Walt Dulaney because he felt a lack in his social capability. This lack might have been dealt with in a variety of ways. A common approach employs a variant of the Socratic method, in which a teacher uses questions as a means of helping his pupil arrive at his own solution to a problem. Walt Dulaney, realizing that Joe was probably well aware of what had to be done but didn't know how to do it, wisely supplied a model that Joe could build on in solving his problem. When an individual knows what response is needed in a given situation but doesn't know how to make that response or can't bring himself to make it, then modeling and role-playing procedures, such as those described in this pamphlet, can provide needed information and practice. Learning the use of the Socratic method in the classroom can be aided by the opportunity to observe a model (an effective teacher) who is skillful in the use of the method.

GLOSSARY

Ambivalence. The coexistence within an individual of opposed attitudes, values or feelings (e.g., love -- hate).

Assertive Training. Teaching an individual through modeling and role-playing (behavior rehearsal) to behave in a more effective, self-confident manner.

Behavior. Any observable, therefore recordable action. (A child speaks or stands or writes an answer. The teacher smiles or reprimands or ignores.)

Behavioral Rehearsal. Imitative role playing of modeled behavior following its observation.

Feedback. Information or reports of the effects of one's behavior on other persons.

Imitation. The act of copying or mimicking the behavior of another person

Identification. A process through which a person becomes similar to or alike another in some way(s).

Model. A person who serves as a source of behavioral cues or information which can be learned or acquired by observers.

Modeling. A process in which one person (observer) learns a new behavior or changes an existing one as a result of observing the behavior of another person (model).

Modeling, Symbolic. Observational learning in which the model is presented via a medium, such as television, motion pictures or drawings, rather than in person.

Observational Learning. See modeling.

Punishment. A negative or aversive event (stimulus) which reduces the likelihood of recurrence of a given behavior.

Recidivism. The repetition of recurrence of deviant behavior, committing a crime upon release from prison.

Reinforcement (negative). The withdrawal or withholding of a reward or positively reinforcing stimulus which reduces the likelihood of recurrence of a given behavior.

Reinforcement (positive). A reward. A stimulus or event (e.g., food, money, praise) which follows a response and increases the likelihood that the response will again occur.

SELECTED BIBLIOGRAPHY

Bandura, A. Principles of behavior modification. New York: Holt,
Rinehart, and Winston, 1969.

A comprehensive review and analysis of the scientific literature
on modeling and observational learning. The focus is more on
psychological experimentation than on classroom applications.
Especially valuable for the reader who wants to find out about the
hard data on which applications of modeling are based.

Chesler, M., and Fox, R. Role-playing methods in the classroom. Chicago:
Science Research Associates, 1966.

A theoretical and practical guide to the use of role-playing in
school settings.

Corsini, R. J., Shaw, M., and Blake, R. R. Role-playing in business and
industry. Glencoe, Illinois: Free Press, 1961.

A manual of role-playing techniques. While aimed at industrial application, it can provide school personnel food for thought.

Gordon, J., Bertcher, H. J., Hayes, M. E., Lawson, M., and Munsey, J. P.
Simulation and imitation: A workbook guide to accompany five self-
instructional audiotapes. Ann Arbor, Michigan: Manpower Science
Services, 1967.

This guidebook with accompanying tapes provide a clear, step-by-step
introduction to modeling and role-playing. Oriented primarily toward
vocational situations and work problems, but a useful source of
techniques for educational workers.

Krumboltz, J. D., and Thoresen, C. E. (Eds.) Behavior counseling: Case
and techniques. New York: Holt, Rinehart, and Winston, 1969.

A collection of articles dealing with the application of behavioral
principles to school settings. Emphasis on methods available to
school counselors.

McDonald, F. J. Behavior modification in teacher education. In National
Society for the Study of Education Yearbook (in press).

A thoughtful, comprehensive treatment of behavior principles, including observational learning, in the training of teachers.

Sarason, I. G., and Ganzer, V. J. Social influence techniques in clinical
and community psychology. In C. D. Spielberger (Ed.) Current topics
in clinical and community psychology. Vol. 1. New York: Academic
Press, 1969, pp. 1-66.

An article that deals with applications of modeling and role-playing to clinical, community, and educational settings.

Sarason, I. G., Glaser, E. M., and Fargo, G. A. Reinforcing productive classroom behavior. U. S. Office of Education Prep Packet. Also published by Behavioral Publications, New York, 1971.

A review of behavior modification principles and how they are applied in schools.

REFERENCES

Carlson, P. K. An analysis of the motor, cognitive, and physiological components of psychotherapeutically induced change in phobic behavior. Unpublished Ph.D. thesis, University of Washington, 1969.

Feshbach, N. D., & Feshbach, S. Imitation of teacher preferences in a field setting. Developmental Psychology, 1972, 7, 84.

Flanagan, J. Functional education for the Seventies. Phi Delta Kappan, Sept. 1967, 27-33.

Jablonsky, A. There are some good teachers of the disadvantaged. IRCD Bulletin, March 1972, 8, 13-17.

McFall, R. M., & Lillesand, D. B. Behavior rehearsal with modeling and coaching in assertion training. Journal of Abnormal Psychology, 1971, 77, 313-323.

Rose, S. D. Treating children in groups. San Francisco: Jossey-Bass, 1972, (especially 106-127).

Sarason, I. G., & Ganzer, V. J. Modeling: An approach to the rehabilitation of juvenile offenders. Final Report to Social and Rehabilitation Service of Department of Health, Education, and Welfare, 1971. (Grant number 15-P-55303).

Stumphauzer, J. S. Increased delay of gratification in young prison inmates through imitation of high-delay peer models. Journal of Personality and Social Psychology, 1972, 21, 10-17.

Vriend, T. J. High performing inner-city adolescents assist low-performing peers in counseling groups. Personnel and Guidance Journal. 1969, 47, 897-904.

Woody, R. M. Behavioral problem children in the schools: Recognition, diagnosis, and behavioral modification. New York: Appleton-Century-Crofts, 1969.

23-402